Courteous Kids

Taking Turns

By Janine Amos   Illustrated by Annabel Spenceley
Consultant Rachael Underwood

Gareth Stevens Publishing
A WORLD ALMANAC EDUCATION GROUP COMPANY

Please visit our web site at: www.garethstevens.com
For a free color catalog describing Gareth Stevens Publishing's
list of high-quality books and multimedia programs,
call 1-800-542-2595 (USA) or 1-800-387-3178 (Canada).
Gareth Stevens Publishing's fax: (414) 332-3567.

Library of Congress Cataloging-in-Publication Data

Amos, Janine.
　　Taking turns / by Janine Amos; illustrated by Annabel Spenceley.
　　　　p. cm. — (Courteous kids)
　　Includes bibliographical references.
　　Summary: Provides examples and tips for working things out when two
people want the same thing.
　　ISBN 0-8368-3173-X (lib. bdg.)
　　　　1. Courtesy—Juvenile literature.　[1. Etiquette.　2. Conduct of life.]
　　I. Spenceley, Annabel, ill.　II. Title.
　　BJ1533.C9A467　2002
　　177'.1—dc21
　　　　　　　　　　　　　　　　　　　　　　　2002017716

This edition first published in 2002 by
Gareth Stevens Publishing
A World Almanac Education Group Company
330 West Olive Street, Suite 100
Milwaukee, Wisconsin　53212　USA

Gareth Stevens editor: JoAnn Early Macken
Cover Design: Katherine A. Goedheer

This edition © 2002 by Gareth Stevens, Inc. First published by Cherrytree Press,
a subsidiary of Evans Brothers Limited.　© 1997 by Cherrytree (a member of the
Evans Group of Publishers), 2A Portman Mansions, Chiltern Street, London
W1M 1LE, United Kingdom.　This U.S. edition published under license from
Evans Brothers Limited.　Additional end matter © 2002 by Gareth Stevens, Inc.

Printed in the United States of America

1 2 3 4 5 6 7 8 9 06 05 04 03 02

Note to Parents and Teachers

The questions that appear in **boldface** type can be used to initiate
discussion with your children or class.　Encourage them to think of
possible answers before continuing with the story.

Ben and Tim

Ben is going to ride the bike.

Tim wants the bike.

Tim pushes Ben off and takes the bike.

How do you think Ben feels?
How do you think Tim feels?

7

Ben cries.

What do you think will happen next?

Ben grabs the bike back from Tim.

Tim and Ben shout at each other.

Jill hurries over to them.
"You look upset, Ben," says Jill.

"And, Tim, you seem angry," she says.

"I want the bike!" says Tim.

"I was on the bike, and you pushed me off.
You shouldn't do that!" says Ben.

15

Ben and Tim both want the bike.
What could they do?

"Tim can have the bike after I
finish my turn," says Ben.

17

"I'll ride around three times," Ben tells Tim.
"Then you can have a turn."

"Okay," Tim agrees. "I'll count."

Ben and Tim have worked out the problem.
Ben takes a turn on the bike.

Now it's Tim's turn.

Ben and Tim each have had a turn riding the bike.
How is Ben feeling now? How is Tim feeling?

22

Maria and Kate

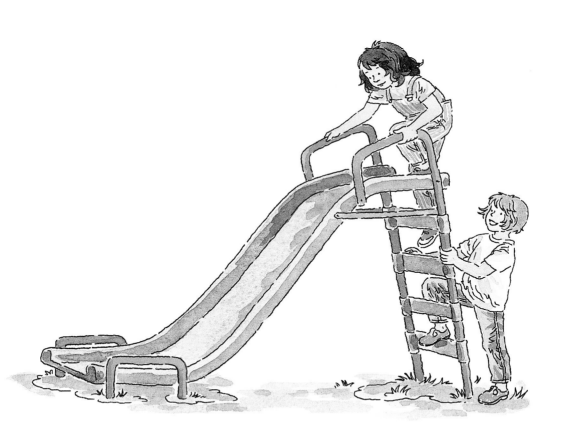

Maria is going down the slide.
She is sliding on her tummy.

Kate wants to slide, too. "Hurry up!" calls Kate.
What do you think will happen next?

25

Kate starts going down the slide.
Maria is still on the slide.

Kate slides into Maria!

"That hurt me!" says Maria.
"It hurt me, too!" says Kate.

What could Kate and Maria do the next time to work out the problem?

The next time, Maria waves to Kate
when she has finished her turn.

Kate waits until Maria is off the slide.

Sometimes, two people want the same thing, but they have a problem when they want it at the same time. They should work out the problem together. When you want a turn at something, tell the other person. Ask when that person will be finished. Then, wait. Your turn will come soon.

More Books to Read

It's My Turn! David Bedford (Tiger Tales)

Me First. Helen Lester (Houghton Mifflin)

Mind Your Manners! Peggy Parish (Mulberry Books)